SUPERPOWER DOGS

HENRY

AVALANCHE RESCUE DOG

SUPERPOWER DOGS

HENRY

AVALANCHE RESCUE DOG

Text by
STEPHANIE PETERS

Little, Brown and Company
New York Boston

Copyright © 2019 by Cosmic Picture Limited

Interior photographs on page 123 copyright © the Bunbury family. Interior photograph on page 124 copyright © Ian Cruickshank. Interior photograph on page 125 copyright © 2019 by Danny Wilcox Frazier VII, for Cosmic Picture Limited.

Front Cover Key Art and Title Treatment copyright © 2019 by Phil Tifo, for Cosmic Picture Limited. Cover photo of background © SaniaTek/Shutterstock.com. Cover photo of flare © kagankiris/Shutterstock.com. IMAX® is a registered trademark of IMAX Corporation. Cover design by Neil Swaab. Cover copyright © 2019 by Hachette Book Group, Inc.

Hachette Book Group supports the right to free expression and the value of copyright. The purpose of copyright is to encourage writers and artists to produce the creative works that enrich our culture.

The scanning, uploading, and distribution of this book without permission is a theft of the author's intellectual property. If you would like permission to use material from the book (other than for review purposes), please contact permissions@hbgusa.com. Thank you for your support of the author's rights.

Little, Brown and Company
Hachette Book Group
1290 Avenue of the Americas, New York, NY 10104
Visit us at LBYR.com

First Edition: June 2019

Little, Brown and Company is a division of Hachette Book Group, Inc.
The Little, Brown name and logo are trademarks of Hachette Book Group, Inc.

The publisher is not responsible for websites (or their content) that are not owned by the publisher.

Library of Congress Control Number: 2019933520

ISBNs: 978-0-316-45362-2 (pbk.), 978-0-316-45360-8 (ebook)

Printed in the United States of America

LSC-C

10 9 8 7 6 5 4 3

HENRY

AVALANCHE RESCUE DOG

The border collie sat high atop the snow-covered hill, his wide triangular ears pricked forward and honey-gold eyes trained on a tiny figure dressed in red far below. When the person moved, the dog stood in anticipation. Watching, waiting. Listening. Then—

"This way!"

The command, distant but clear, sent a jolt of electricity through the dog's sleek body. He burst into a full-on sprint.

One-two. Three-four. One-two. Three-four.

His big paws touched down in a steady four-count rhythm. His muscular legs stretched out and pulled back, the long strides propelling him forward over the crusty snowpack. His furry reddish-brown head bobbed in time with his footfalls. His curved white-tipped tail waved like a banner behind him.

One-two. Three-four. One-two. Three-four.

As he ran, he left a single skinny track in the fresh snow, like a pencil slowly tracing a line on a clean, white sheet of paper. Short at first but longer by the second.

One-two. Three-four. One-two. Three-four.

Rocks and boulders peeked out of the snow. The dog veered around one, dodged past another, and sailed over a third with a mighty bound, weaving around the obstacles but never straying off course.

One-two. Three-four. One-two. Three-four.

His shadow kept pace with him as he raced down the slope toward the figure in red. Mouth open, he tasted the crisp mountain air on his tongue and smelled the scent of snow, ice, evergreen, and rock with every breath.

Panting hard now. Tiring.

One…two. Three…four. One…two. Three…four.

Slowing. But not stopping.

One. Two. Three. Four. One. Two. Three. Four.

Every step bringing him closer and closer and closer until—

"Good dog!" The figure in red, a compactly built man with a salt-and-pepper beard and a mile-wide grin of delight, crouched as the dog reached him. He swept his pup into a bear hug and ruffled his silky ears with a gloved hand, then looked to the far-off hilltop where the border collie had begun his run. "Now, that's what I call a long-distance recall!" He chuckled. "You know how many dogs would stay on task from way up there to way down here? Not many. They'd get distracted and wander off." He stroked the white fur on his dog's neck. "But not you, huh, boy?"

Still panting, the dog gazed at him with adoring eyes. The man gazed back and smiled. "You're such a good dog, Henry," he murmured. "Is there anything you can't do?"

Henry tilted his head back, pink nostrils twitching. Newly fallen snow coated the ski trail in front of him. More snow was on the way, his nose told him. His whole body detected it, in fact, for exposed to the elements as it was, it registered even the subtlest changes in the weather.

"Henry!"

Henry snapped to attention at the sound of his human's voice. Ian Bunbury, professional ski patroller and a handler and trainer with the Canadian Avalanche Rescue Dog Association (CARDA), stood farther down the trail. His goggles rested on his forehead, his ski helmet snug over his graying hair, and his bright red ski patrol jacket brilliant against the white snow. Henry locked eyes with him. Then Ian lowered his goggles and pushed off on his skis.

"This way!"

Like an arrow released from a bow, Henry streaked after him. Without slowing or stopping, Ian widened his stance. Henry darted between his legs, his floppy red-brown ears streaming behind him and his paws churning up the new snow as they dug down to the groomed trail beneath. His lungs filled with fresh mountain air and his ears with the gentle whisper from Ian's skis moving through the snow. As they headed down the slope, he felt Ian's fingers brush the back handle of his red-and-black K9 Storm vest, but he didn't break stride. They moved as a single graceful unit—Henry beneath and between Ian's legs—curving in wide arcs down the mountainside.

Midway down the trail, Ian cruised to a stop, then skied off to inspect a large fir tree. The evergreen's branches were weighed down by the previous night's snowfall. They drooped to the ground and formed a tent that hid the area surrounding the tree's trunk. More snow ringed the outside of the tent in mounds.

"That looks like a tree well," Ian muttered as he

withdrew his collapsible avalanche probe from his daypack. To Henry, he said, "Down."

Henry plopped onto his belly as Ian snapped the probe into a single three-meter (ten-foot) pole. Jabbing the probe into the snow, Ian edged cautiously toward the tree. At first, the probe hit layers of old, packed snow lying just beneath the new layer of white. But when Ian pushed aside some branches and stabbed again, the probe buried itself halfway up to his hand.

Ian quickly backed away. The branches swung back into place, shedding snow in clumps. He pulled out his handheld radio. "Dispatch, I'm here on Bears' Den, and I'm noticing the tree wells are starting to get pretty significant," he said when the radio crackled to life. "If someone falls headfirst into one, it could be bad. Henry and I are going to check the rest of the trail, then come in."

Ian holstered his radio, returned to the trail, and bent down. "Up!"

With one smooth motion, Henry leaped onto Ian's back and settled like a scarf around his shoulders. Ian hooked a finger under the collar of Henry's vest. "Ready?"

Woof!

From his perch, Henry scented the air as they swooshed down the slope. The smell of humans, exhaust fumes from snowmobiles, whiffs of food—his super sensitive nostril receptors, three hundred million of them (fifty times more than humans have), detected them all. He switched from riding to running, sometimes between Ian's legs and other times far to his side, away from the sharp edges of his skis, always dropping into a downstay when Ian stopped to deal with minor problems. A frayed section of rope in the rope-and-bamboo boundary fence. A trail sign turned invisible by a thick, icy crust. A plastic water bottle, its contents frozen solid, dropped or left behind by a careless skier. Another tree well.

At the slope's end, Henry hopped up next to Ian on the chairlift. The padded seat was cozy, and Ian's hand on his neck was warm and soothing. The lift ferried them high above the skiers to the Whistler Mountain alpine area, where they made their way to a large gray building with a bright red PATROL sign above the main entrance. Inside, Henry padded after Ian through the main room into the rescue room.

★**8**★

Two kennels sat amid carefully stored emergency gear. Still wearing his K9 Storm vest, Henry went straight into his crate, turned in a circle, and laid his head on his paws. Familiar sounds washed over him—the murmur of human activity mingled with the hum of machines—and he let out a contented huff.

Then the sounds changed. Henry perked up, ears forward, listening.

Ian's and others' voices rose with sudden urgency. Boots hammered back and forth across the concrete floor. Then one set of footsteps thudded in his direction.

AVALANCHE 411

It's early winter and the first snowfall of the season drifts down from the sky onto a mountain. The ground is frozen, so the flakes stick and coat the slope with a thin mantle of white. In the days that follow, other storms lay down more snow of different consistencies—an inch or two of light powder; a crust of sleet; a drizzle of freezing rain; and a heavy, wet snow that weighs down the others. A night of bitter cold freezes the top layers solid. Then—*wham!* An all-day blizzard dumps more than three feet of fluffy powder on top of everything.

That thick new blanket of snow is beautiful. But the snowpack below it is changing. A warming thaw follows a sudden drop in temperature, creating an unstable layer hidden deep beneath the powder. The top blanket clings to the snowpack...until suddenly, and without warning, the snowpack separates from the layers below and releases.

Like a kid shooting down a playground slide, the enormous slab hurtles downhill. In just seconds, its speed jumps from zero to forty, then to sixty, then to eighty or more miles per hour. The slab shatters like a pane of glass as it thunders down the slope, the pieces ripping up debris—rocks and tree limbs and frozen dirt and jagged ice—from the surface. The pounding wave of snow races onward until finally, the avalanche slows, then stops. A silence descends on the mountainside. A cloud of powder drifts away, revealing a widespread pile of debris-filled, concrete-hard chunks of snow.

These types of avalanches are known as slabs. Their size, speed, and suddenness have earned them nicknames such as White Death and the Snowy Torrent. The most catastrophic slab avalanches can bury a mile-wide expanse beneath more than one hundred thousand tons of snow. But other avalanche types are devastating, too. Loose snow avalanches, or sluffs, can be just as big and powerful as slabs. As they spread out in a widening fan shape from their starting point, sluffs can easily drag a skier through trees, over cliffs, or into other deadly terrain. Frozen waterfalls, known as icefalls, and snow cornices created by the winter winds can break free and trigger avalanches on the slopes below. And don't be fooled by the wet, relatively slow-moving glide avalanches. If the heavy slush of these slides swamps your skis, you'll be stuck just as if you'd stepped into wet cement.

Obviously, the best way to avoid being caught in an avalanche is to stay away from avalanche-prone areas in the backcountry. Such areas are clearly marked with boundary fences and are monitored by the mountain's expert ski patrollers for any signs of danger. Those who do choose to ski those backcountry slopes should obey standard backcountry safety rules: Always notify the ski patrol where you'll be skiing before you set off. Always ski with a partner or a group. Always ski in sight of at least one other person. And always carry avalanche emergency gear—a collapsible probe and shovel in a daypack and a two-way transceiver on a harness.

"Some skiers resist bringing a daypack," Ian says. "They think it will slow them down or get in the way. Or they figure the probe and shovel will be useless if they get buried by an avalanche, so why bother? Here's what I say to those people: What if you're not the one who's buried? What if it's your friend? Your shovel, probe, and transceiver are your best tools for finding and digging that person free. I'd say the possibility of saving your friend's life is worth a little inconvenience, wouldn't you?"

The hard truth is most people caught in an avalanche won't survive. The cause of death is most often suffocation or impact trauma. Avoidance of avalanche terrain in hazardous conditions is the simplest, most foolproof way of not becoming an avalanche victim. So seek as much local information about the snowpack as you can. Then, if you do ski, snowboard, or snowmobile in the backcountry, understand what you can do to save yourself and others if an avalanche does hit!

AVALANCHE SURVIVAL GUIDELINES:

★ Before the avalanche catches you, scream and yell at the top of your lungs so others in your group will know you're in trouble. Then close your mouth—and keep it closed to prevent ice, snow, and debris from getting in.

★ If you can jump back off the loosening snow onto a stable surface above the break point, do so.

★ Don't try to outrun the slide! Even the best skiers and snowboarders can't move faster than an avalanche. Instead, ski or board sideways, across and out of the avalanche's path.

★ If you can't get out of the path, ditch your poles and skis or snowboard as soon as possible. They can pull you down and under the snow and make your arms and legs twist violently, leading to injury. But hang on to your emergency equipment!

★ If you can, grab onto a tree or a boulder to anchor yourself in place, then ride out the avalanche there.

★ Use swimming motions to keep yourself above or near the avalanche's surface. The closer you are to the top of the snow, the faster rescuers—including avalanche rescue dogs like Henry—can find you and dig you out.

★ If at all possible, cup one hand or arm around your nose and mouth to create an air pocket and push your other arm through the surface so others can see it.

THIRTY MINUTES REMAINING...

"Code A!"

A rush of adrenaline washed through Ian's system. Code A meant someone had been involved in an avalanche. *Involved* as in lost beneath the heavy, concrete-hard snow.

As a member of the ski patrol, he handled different emergencies—falls on the slopes, medical problems, missing persons—all the time. But a Code A callout was rare. Whistler Mountain Ski Patrol made sure of that. Their highly trained avalanche forecasters regularly monitored the mountain's acres of snowpack. When they identified an avalanche-prone area, their team of trained avalanche control technicians defused the threat by skiing or helicoptering to the site, clearing that space, and lobbing small bombs at targeted spots in the snow. The explosions triggered a controlled slide. Such preventive measures removed most avalanche risks.

Most, but not all. That's why Ian and Henry trained constantly—so when an avalanche with involvement occurred, they would be prepared to act. To save the life of a person buried beneath the snow, the ultimate mission of all CARDA teams.

"Code A!" the dispatcher called again.

Ski patrollers were already in motion, heading toward their lockers for their gear. Ian hadn't shed any of his layers or shelved his equipment since coming off the slopes. He hadn't had time.

Time. Statistically speaking, a person buried by an avalanche had a 90 percent chance of survival if found within fifteen to eighteen minutes. After thirty minutes, the person's air supply would have dwindled to dangerously low levels, and their chance of survival plummeted to 30 percent. Also after thirty minutes, the likelihood that they'd be found alive was slim to none.

The ski patrol's clock read 14:36. Like all emergency services, they used twenty-four-hour military time because it was more precise than the standard twelve-hour clock, where 9:00 could be either morning or night. Recorded in military time, there was no question when an event happened.

Ian did a quick mental calculation. Thirty minutes from now was 15:06—3:06 p.m. in standard time. They needed to find the avalanche victim before then. *Long* before then, if possible.

He crossed to the rescue room in big strides. Henry was already on his feet, ears pricked and eyes searching. Ian knew his dog's senses were far better than any human's, so Henry had likely registered his footsteps and the surge of activity in the other room. He bet Henry had picked up on the sudden spike in emotions, too. Dogs who were tuned in to human moods, as his border collie was, could sense when those moods abruptly changed.

"This way, Henry!"

Side by side, they hurried into the ski patrol's main room. The "bump" room, as it was better known, was so nicknamed because a patroller coming off the mountain "bumped" the next patroller on duty out onto the slopes. Gathered in the bump room now were the three other members of the rescue team: Tom and Bob, the two searchers, and Jan, the avalanche fore-caster and field rescue leader. Jan's job was to assess the site and determine whether conditions were safe enough to mount a search. She would look for "hang fire"—unstable snowpack that could suddenly release in a second avalanche and endanger the searchers. Until she gave the all clear, the signal that the area was safe, no one on the team would be allowed onto the avalanche debris pile. She'd call off the search alto-gether rather than risk her teammates' lives.

Ian hoped his friend wouldn't have to make that call today.

"Transport's on its way," the dispatcher reported.

"Then let's get a move on," Jan said.

Ian shouldered his daypack and called for Henry to follow him. The others parted to let their canine teammate pass. Everyone recognized how vital he was to their efforts. As skilled as they were, they couldn't do what Henry could. With nimble-footed agility, Henry could cover more ground in thirty minutes than a team of ten searchers could cover in four hours. His supersensitive nose would sift through smells

★18★

only he could detect, searching for the unique scent of a human buried beneath the snow. And with single-minded focus and the drive to work, he'd keep searching for that smell until he found the source or Ian called him off.

The frigid air hit Ian like a slap in the face when he stepped outside. Winter temperatures on Whistler Mountain often hovered around freezing or below, and this afternoon was no exception. He'd learned long ago that wearing multiple layers of wool and lightweight, insulating fabrics helped keep the dangerous cold at bay.

He wished everyone who visited the mountain knew to protect themselves that way.

"Time?" Jan asked.

Ian checked his watch and grimaced. "14:40."

Four minutes had already ticked by, leaving the thirty-minute countdown at twenty-six. And their transport was nowhere in sight.

WHISTLER AND CARDA QUESTIONS AND ANSWERS

The histories of Whistler Mountain and the Canadian Avalanche Rescue Dog Association, or CARDA, are intertwined. But which came first, and how did the two come to be connected? To learn more about where Henry and Ian live, work, and play and the organization they're part of, read on!

Q: How did Whistler Mountain become a ski resort?

A: Whistler Mountain wasn't always the premier ski destination it is today. Long before skiers, snowmobilers, and snowboarders took to the slopes, the region was inhabited by people from the Squamish and Lil'wat First Nations. The peak came to the attention of Europeans in the mid-1860s, when surveyors from the British Navy dubbed it London Mountain. But most settlers who arrived in the years that followed called it Whistler after the shrill sound made by the western hoary marmots that live there.

Back then, Whistler was frequented only by the hardiest outdoor adventurers, prospectors in search of gold, and trappers looking to make money on the fur trade. That changed in the early 1900s, when a small fishing lodge opened its doors on Whistler's Alta Lake. With each passing year, the lodge drew in more visitors. By 1920, it had ballooned into a resort that could accommodate more than one hundred people.

Still, the mountain might have remained undeveloped if not for the Olympics. In 1960, the Olympic Committee considered Whistler as a possible location for the 1968 Winter Games. Although that opportunity fell through, a chairlift company recognized the mountain's potential as a top-notch tourist location. From 1962 to 1965, it installed T-bars, chairlifts, and a state-of-the-art gondola that could ferry four people up the mountain in an enclosed cabin that hung below a cable. The company also built its own lodge and carved out six ski trails on Whistler's slopes.

When the new resort area opened for business in 1966, recreational skiers arrived in droves. As its popularity grew, the resort added more lifts, trails, hotels, and amenities. Whistler Mountain chairlifts can now accommodate nearly thirty-five thousand skiers *per hour.*

And in 2010, Whistler finally got its chance to host events during the Winter Olympic Games. Today, five stacked stone statues named Inukshuk—an Inuit term for this kind of landmark—proudly overlook the summit.

Q: What is the connection between Whistler Mountain and CARDA?

A: The Canadian Avalanche Rescue Dog Association was founded by veteran Whistler Mountain ski patroller Bruce Watt. Watt was caught in an avalanche in 1978. He was one of the lucky ones: he survived. But like other ski patrollers and rescue personnel, he believed that canine searchers were the key to improving other people's chances in the future. So when Whistler Mountain asked him to organize a volunteer canine program, he accepted. CARDA was officially formed in 1982 with the mission of saving the lives of avalanche victims by training and maintaining dog-and-handler search and rescue teams throughout the mountainous and avalanche-prone regions of western Canada. Today,

Whistler Mountain is one of several CARDA training sites; its ski patrol has six validated CARDA teams, the largest number of any ski resort in Canada. Ian and Henry make up one of those teams.

Q: Can anyone with a dog be a handler for CARDA?

A: In a word, no. To qualify as a CARDA handler, a person must be certified in first aid and CPR, be an expert backcountry skier, and be willing and able to dedicate two or more years to developing a dog into a search and rescue canine—and then continue training with the dog throughout its eight to ten years in service. CARDA teams must be available to respond to callouts at a moment's notice, so living near and working at a mountain ski resort is highly advantageous. Unsurprisingly, the best handler candidates are usually members of a ski patrol. And obviously, a love of dogs is absolutely necessary!

Q: What's the best age to begin training a dog for avalanche search and rescue work?

A: CARDA accepts new canine recruits who are between six months and two years old. If younger than that, the puppy might not be ready, physically or mentally, for the hard work ahead. If older than two years, the dog will have too few years to work before reaching retirement age. Plus, an older dog could have formed some habits that don't suit search and rescue work. Better to let that dog continue life as a beloved pet.

Q: How does a puppy get into the CARDA program?

A: Every May, CARDA holds a three-day-long evaluation of new puppies and their handlers. Like a young athlete trying out for a sports team, the puppy is put through a series of simple drills and exercises. Evaluators observe the puppy's behavior and determine if it is a good match for the program. Does the puppy show excitement when asked to do something, or does it hold back? Is the puppy focused on the task at hand or easily distracted? Does it have a strong bond with its handler? If the puppy and its handler pass CARDA's spring assessment, then they are granted potential Team in Training status.

Q: What happens once a puppy gets accepted into the program?

A: Potential Teams in Training attend the puppy, or beginner, division of CARDA's winter course in January. Here, the puppy learns to channel its natural hunting drive toward a new goal: the hunt for human scent. The teams practice finding live quarries—humans hiding in snow caves, known as quinzees, or in shallow trenches beneath a thin layer of snow. The searches gradually increase in difficulty throughout the week. Early on, the quarry is the dog's handler, the quinzee or trench is close by, and some part of the quarry is visible. Later, the dog searches for a stranger hidden in a more distant cave. Puppies and handlers who perform well during the week earn their "In Training" certificate and the right to attend the next year's winter session, where they will undergo their validation test.

Q: Are there training sessions between the first and second winter courses?

A: Teams in Training are encouraged to attend the spring course and have their progress assessed, but most of the training during the gap—the time between the winter sessions—is done on the handler's own time. It's really important that the team constantly hones its skills because the dog-and-handler pair will undergo a challenging validation test at its second winter course. Only validated teams are added to CARDA's roster for callouts—and only teams that dedicate themselves to the training are likely to be validated.

Q: So, a dog with the right skills will always be validated?

A: Skills are important, of course, but so is the dog's drive to work. CARDA has nicknames for the dogs with this winning combination. "Barn Burners" are the absolute cream of the crop—fast, persistent, and always excited and raring to go. "Solids" are speedy, dedicated all-around searchers, reliable, and good at what they do. Unfortunately, there are also the "Seventy-Five Per-centers": dogs that will do what they're trained to do, but only 75 percent of the time. The rest of the time, they show little to no interest in the work. Chances are, these dogs will be cut from the program because someday, their refusal to do their job could cost an avalanche victim's life.

Q: Does training end after the dog earns its validation?

A: Training is a lifelong commitment, both for the dog and for the handler. They do most of it on their own, but validated teams can also practice their skills with other validated teams in the advanced group during CARDA's winter session. Or they can sign up for a special weeklong advanced course in early spring that puts experienced teams through challenging backcountry rescue scenarios.

Q: Where can I find more information?

A: Ask your parents for permission to check out the websites for Whistler Mountain, CARDA, and other avalanche rescue dog sites!

TWENTY-SIX MINUTES REMAINING...

Henry's gaze darted from Ian to the other ski patrollers. In the Alpine Service Building moments before, they'd moved like a well-oiled machine, pulling equipment from lockers, hooks, and shelves and stuffing their bodies into their bright red turnout gear. *It's go time,* their body language proclaimed, *and we're ready for what's ahead.*

But here at the edge of the snow-covered clearing, they were harder to read. They stood in a tight cluster, not moving except to shuffle their feet or shade their eyes and stare at the sky.

"It's taking longer than usual," Tom muttered. "Time's running—"

Chop-chop-chop-chop-chop!

Henry swiveled his head skyward in sync with the ski patrollers. From a distant horizon, a helicopter emerged from the clouds. It looked as small as a mosquito at first but quickly grew larger as it approached—larger, and louder, the rhythmic beat of the rotors cutting through the still air. The sound hammered into Henry's sensitive ears as the craft made a quick first pass over the clearing, circled back, and started its descent.

As the helicopter neared the ground, it kicked up a tornado of snow. Henry ducked his head against the powdery onslaught. The noise, the snow flurry, the sheer magnitude of the machine dropping out of the sky right in front of him—the instinct to run was powerful. But his self-control was stronger. And his trust in Ian was absolute. His handler had brought him here, and Ian would never knowingly put him in harm's way. Therefore, he was safe.

So, like Ian and the other humans around him, Henry stood his ground. Patient and unmoving, even when the chopper touched down, its nose just a few feet away and pointed right at him. Still, he wagged his tail when the engine cut off and the deafening noise was replaced by the gentler *whoosh-whoosh-whoosh* of the slowing rotors.

When the rotors stopped, the ski patrollers surged forward. Tom beelined to the right and started piling the search party's skis and gear into a long container attached to the outside of the helicopter. Bob climbed up into the cabin and held out his arms.

"Give him here, Ian!"

Henry felt a light tug on his K9 Storm vest. Suddenly, he was in the air, legs dangling, as Ian passed him up to a waiting teammate. Ian swung in after him a moment later, scooped Henry into his arms, and took a seat.

"Good dog," he murmured as he strapped himself in. "Good dog."

Even separated by Ian's layers of clothing and his own vest, Henry felt his handler's voice rumble against his chest. He tilted his head back, gazed at Ian, and gave a low woof in response. Then, with a swipe of his tongue, he licked melting snow off his chops and settled more comfortably onto Ian's lap.

Everyone else strapped into their seats, Jan in

★31★

front next to the pilot, Bob and Tom behind with Ian. The pilot flicked some switches. The engine roared back to life, sending violent vibrations thrumming through the cabin floor and up into Henry's body. As the rotors whirled faster and faster, another blizzard spun up around them, blurring the view with a cloud of white.

Then the pilot pulled on a lever, and the chopper slowly lifted straight up off the snow. Henry stilled, nostrils twitching. Outside the plexiglass windows, skinny fir trees flapped their branches in the sudden windstorm. He caught whiffs of evergreen and snow mixed with the helicopter's exhaust fumes and the rich, warm smell of humans. Then the treetops gave way to dull gray sky and the helicopter shifted from vertical to forward motion. Within seconds, they'd left the clearing behind and were soaring high over the Whistler Mountain summit.

"14:44," Ian announced over the high-pitched whine of the helicopter's engines.

Henry raised his head. He didn't understand the words. But Ian's tone, the tension in his muscles, and the tightness around his lips told him something important was happening. Something that he—that they—were part of.

He licked his chops again and laid his head in the crook of Ian's elbow. He didn't know what that something was or where they were going. But instinct and experience told him that when they got there, he'd need all his energy. He rested now so he'd be ready then.

HENRY'S "DAD"

Skiing, search and rescue, and dogs: all three have been part of Ian Bunbury's life for as long as he can remember.

"I grew up skiing the slopes of Whistler," he says. "We'd drive straight from North Vancouver after school on Friday, stay in one of the cabins my dad built, and ski until it was time to return home on Sunday."

Ian's father, Alex, was a well-known figure in the Whistler community. In the 1960s, he helped survey the area for the future ski resort, then bought ten acres of land and built three rustic cabins there. He also volunteered for both the Whistler Mountain Ski Patrol and the North Shore Rescue (NSR), an all-volunteer search and rescue organization.

"Dad would come home from his regular job at weird times, grab his pack, and be gone for hours on a callout, then return exhausted in the middle of the night," Ian recalls of his father's volunteer duties.

He also remembers a time when he got to help out

during an NSR training exercise. "I played a missing child getting rescued. This big muscular guy strapped me to his back, and we rappelled down a mountain cliff. It was scary, but I had total confidence in him. And I was really proud to be part of that training."

It was through NSR that twelve-year-old Ian met his first search and rescue dog, a German shepherd named Alu. Alu was titled by the American Kennel Club as a Tracking Dog Excellent, or TDX, and he made a big impression on Ian.

"My family had dogs all my life, but I'd never interacted with one who responded to commands the way Alu did. I was fascinated by the sense of teamwork, the give and take, the *purposefulness* of the relationship. I knew that someday, I wanted to own a dog like that."

Alex was impressed by Alu's abilities, too. So he got a dog of his own, a female German shepherd named Bebe, and trained her to be a tracker. Once again, Ian got to help. "Dad would take me up the mountain, then tell me to 'get lost'—to hide in the woods. Sometime later, Bebe would come crashing through the brush and find me. It was fun." He pauses, reflecting. "I didn't really think about it

then, but sitting alone in the woods, in the quiet…
I learned that I could be okay by myself, that I didn't
always need an adult watching over me."

When Alu and Bebe had a litter, Alex let Ian pick
a pup for himself. Ian gave the little German shepherd a good German name: Fritz.

"I trained Fritz as best I could," Ian remembers,
"but really, I wasn't sure what I was doing. Still, he
was a great dog. I had him until I was in my late
teens."

By that time, Ian was living the "ski bum" life in
the family's cabin on Whistler. He worked as a ski
instructor and, later, as a coach for several different
alpine ski racing teams. Then in 1990, the team he
was coaching abruptly folded. That's when the Whistler Mountain assistant ski patrol director invited
him to join the patrol.

With his skiing expertise, understanding of emergency procedures, and knowledge of the mountain,
Ian was perfectly suited for the position. But he
longed to expand his role. "The first thing I asked
was, Can I get into the canine program?"

In the early 1980s, Whistler and other ski patrols
had incorporated a new program into their emergency

services: the Canadian Avalanche Rescue Dog Association, or CARDA. Dog-and-handler pairs underwent two or more years of rigorous training aimed at teaching dogs to locate victims buried beneath avalanches. Ian knew all about CARDA, having been at Whistler when the association was founded. He'd watched it grow with great interest, and now he wanted to be a part of it.

Unfortunately, the program was so popular, there were no available spots. Ian didn't let that deter him. He put his name on the waiting list, then tagged along with those going through the training to see what it was all about. He even volunteered to play the quarry, sitting alone in a snow cave for long stretches of time and waiting patiently for a dog to find him— the snowy version of the exercise he'd once done with Bebe.

Three years went by. Finally, in 1993, Ian's patience paid off. A space in the CARDA program opened up and was offered to him. It was time to get a puppy.

TWENTY-TWO MINUTES REMAINING...

As the helicopter flew over the ski resort, Ian had a flashback to a gondola ride he and Henry had taken when Henry was just a pup. As a search and rescue (SAR) dog, Henry needed to be at ease riding in and on many different vehicles—not just trucks and cars, but gondolas, chairlifts, snowmobiles, toboggans, helicopters, and more. The sooner he was exposed to each of them, the better.

To make Henry's first gondola ride even more interesting, Ian selected a cabin with a window in the floor. Some people love the bird's-eye view of the snowy valley passing below them; others find it a bit unnerving. As their cabin swept out of the station, Ian wondered how Henry would react.

The puppy immediately flattened himself down on his front legs on top of the window. With his rear end high and his tail wagging, he scanned the terrain passing beneath them. Seconds later, he leaped up. Barking excitedly, eyes trained on the ground below, he bounced on his front paws. Then he craned his neck to look up at Ian and barked again. *What else you got?* his body language and bark seemed to say.

Well, he's got energy, that's for sure, Ian had thought then, smiling down at his pup. *And he seems curious, not intimidated or scared. Good traits for a dog who's going to have an important job in the future.*

A job that Henry, now grown up and trained, would perform shortly if Jan gave them the thumbs-up to search.

The helicopter passed over a sparse forest that sat smack in the middle of an established avalanche path. Season after season, waves of snow and ice churned through the area. The trees survived, some of them for more than two hundred years, by bending not breaking—a testament to nature's resilience.

They reached their target zone a moment later. Through his helmet headset, Ian heard Bob give a low, awed whistle. "What a *monster.*"

A relative newcomer to the ski patrol, Bob hadn't seen many avalanches. But even Ian, whose experience spanned decades, was taken aback by the sheer magnitude of the slide. The slab had released high up on the mountain, then raced over an outcropping, where it wrenched rocks and branches and other debris from the ground before pounding down into the snowy valley bottom. The debris field looked like a jigsaw puzzle thrown aside by a gigantic hand, the pieces scattered about and piled up in jagged mounds.

The pilot did a flyover so Jan could survey the area for residual hazards. Ian scanned the site, too, not just for hang fire but to get an overall mental picture of the area Henry would be searching.

"Okay, it looks good," Jan declared. "So—"

"I've got a problem," the pilot interrupted. "I don't see a good LZ near the search site."

Ian's lips tightened. Without a suitable LZ, or landing zone, the pilot had a decision to make. He could put the helicopter down in a stable spot farther away. This was the safest option for landing but would cost them precious time, since the rescuers would have to ski back to the avalanche site over potentially dangerous terrain. Or the pilot could fly back to base and reconfigure the helicopter with a long line, then return and lower the rescuers down to the site from a high hover position—a time-consuming operation that posed its own unique set of risks. As someone who had been inserted into rescue sites via long line before, Ian understood that better than some. But if that's what the pilot deemed best—

"I'm going to do a toe-in." The pilot's announcement rang in Ian's ears.

A toe-in was a tricky maneuver that required the pilot to land on just a portion of the helicopter's skids rather than fully on both. With the engines at full power, he'd hold that precarious position as the searchers slowly and carefully disembarked and unloaded their gear. A miscommunication between crewmates, an unexpected shift in weight, even a sudden gust of wind could throw the helicopter off balance. And that could spell disaster for them all.

But with time ticking down—just twenty minutes left by Ian's watch—the toe-in was their best option.

"Do it," Jan said.

As they descended, a rotor-whipped snowstorm blew up around them. With the engines on full, it continued to blow even after the helicopter touched down on the front tips of its skids. "Nice and easy, everyone," the pilot cautioned.

The helicopter bobbed and swayed like a boat on waves as the crew slowly reversed the earlier loading process. Tom exited first, climbing from the doorway to the skid and then easing down to the ground. Jan followed. Then Bob stood up and held out his arms. He'd need to hold Henry while Ian climbed out of the helicopter.

"Whenever you're ready, Ian," he said.

Ian shifted to unbuckle his seat belt. As he did, Henry suddenly sat up. His paws scrabbled for purchase on the smooth surface of Ian's turnout gear. Bob's eyes widened in alarm. If Henry fell—

Ian instinctively tightened his one-armed grip around Henry's belly, securing him. "There's a good dog," he murmured. "Good dog."

★ 43 ★

Ian knew Henry had picked up on the surge in tension. It was up to him to calm Henry back down. Murmured words helped, but his body language spoke even more clearly. So he relaxed his hold. And a moment later, Henry relaxed, too.

"Good dog," Ian said. "Good dog."

SCOUT

Ask people to picture an avalanche rescue dog, and most will describe a shaggy Saint Bernard with a barrel around its neck. And it's true that Saint Bernards once helped save lives in snowy European environments. One dog, Barry der Menschenretter of Switzerland, is credited with rescuing more than forty people from a dangerous mountain pass between 1800 and 1812. Nowadays, though, smaller working breeds, such as German shepherds, border collies, and golden retrievers, have replaced the much bigger Saint Bernards, whose easygoing temperament proved them to be better pets than search partners.

When it came time to find a dog to train as his CARDA partner, Ian immediately thought of German shepherds. After all, Alu, Bebe, and Fritz had been wonderful to work with. But just as quickly, he realized the breed wouldn't be the right fit. "German shepherds are large dogs that can weigh up to eighty pounds. That's just too big, too bulky for the type of work I was going to be doing. No way I could carry such a large dog on my shoulders or see around one sitting in front of me on a snowmobile."

Instead, Ian found a breeder of border collies. Supersmart and medium in size, border collies have great endurance, high tolerance for cold, and rarely experience the chronic physical issues known to plague some other breeds. Most important, border collies are born with a deep-rooted desire to work. From the litter, Ian chose a little black-and-white puppy, who he named Scout. He started Scout off in obedience training, then moved on to the next step: the CARDA spring assessment.

CARDA holds two main sessions a year. The weeklong general winter training course in January is for dog-and-handler teams already accepted into the program and seeking to be validated by CARDA. The three-day spring session in May is when new recruits are assessed for acceptance into the program. "The CARDA testers had to be absolutely sure Scout and I had the right stuff," Ian says. "Otherwise, training us would be a waste of valuable time and resources."

To his delight, he and Scout passed the 1993 spring assessment. During the winter session the following January, they learned the basic skills needed to become a CARDA-validated search and rescue team. More advanced teams were training then, too, giving Ian a glimpse of what his and Scout's future held. At the end of the week, they were presented with their "In Training" certificate, putting them one step closer to their goal. And in 1995, after more than a lot of dedicated, continuous work, Ian and Scout were validated as an official CARDA Avalanche Rescue Dog Team.

"Scout was amazing during the test," Ian says proudly. "In fact, after our validation search, one tester said, 'He's the kind of dog I'd want searching for me.'"

Yet Ian admits he probably should have done some things differently with Scout. "Rescue dogs need to have a strong bond with their handlers. But they also need to be comfortable with strangers. Not so comfortable that they choose to interact with outsiders instead of searching for victims, but not wary of other people, either. But I took an overly protective, 'he's mine' attitude with Scout—didn't want anyone else to come near him. Luckily, it didn't end up being an issue. But it was something I vowed to do differently with my next dog."

Ian learned another valuable lesson during his partnership with Scout.

"Ski patrollers typically ski or snowmobile to emergencies. Both methods are fast and offer the best mobility. But I was an early adopter of snowboarding. The resort wanted to promote the up-and-coming sport. They let me snowboard when I was on duty, so visitors could see it in action."

One afternoon, Ian snowboarded to a work run on the lower beginner slopes of Olympic Station. Scout was resting back in his kennel in the Alpine Service Building. "I finished up and caught a ride on the nearest chairlift, which was also Whistler's slowest. That's when a call came in over the radio. Code A, Flute Basin. And there I was, stuck on the chairlift, my dog and rescue gear far away, and with a snowboard instead of skis."

The memory of missing a chance for a live find still smarts even years later. "I would never want anyone to be in an avalanche just so I could do my job," Ian says. "But as a member of CARDA, my mission is to save the life of a victim. I wasn't ready to do that that day." He pauses. "That was a mistake. Everyone makes mistakes. But it's what you do to recover from them, to move forward…that's what matters."

Since then, Ian has always traveled with his gear and, whenever possible, with his dog. "I swore never to be caught out of position like that again. And I never have been."

TWENTY MINUTES REMAINING...

The noise should have stopped when the helicopter landed. The humans should have already removed their helmets and gotten out. He should be on the snowy ground at Ian's feet, ready and waiting for his handler's first command. That's how these helicopter rides had always ended before.

Instead, with the roar of the engines still in his ears, Henry was in Bob's arms, watching Ian lower himself to the skid with agonizing slowness. First his feet, then his body, and then his head disappeared from view.

A moment later, the helicopter rocked. Not so

violently as to pitch them off balance, yet Bob's arms tightened around him. Henry didn't like being squeezed that way. He wanted to squirm free and jump out the doorway after Ian.

But he didn't. Ian had taught him to remain calm during transitions like this, and that training kicked in now. He was still and quiet as Bob eased to the door, knelt, and gently released him into Ian's waiting arms.

"Good boy," Ian praised as he hurried Henry through the whirling snow and away from the helicopter. "Good boy."

And now Henry did squirm, not with discomfort but with pleasure at the warmth in his handler's familiar tone.

The other searchers joined them, and the helicopter left, taking its deafening *chop-chop-chop* noise and stink of exhaust with it. The blur of snow settled. When it did, Ian crouched, scooped up a handful of fresh powder, and tossed it in the air. Glittering and winking in the pale sunshine, the icy flakes drifted on the breeze across the avalanche's toe. Ian nodded to himself, then clicked into the skis Tom had brought over and reached for his gear.

"Help! Help!"

Henry whipped around at the sound of the scream. A young woman wearing a neon-purple ski jacket and equipped with backcountry touring gear emerged from the rubble at the base of the avalanche. She stumbled over the uneven surface as she ran toward them. "My friend is buried out there!" she cried, gesturing wildly at the avalanche debris. "You've got to find him!"

Sour breath, steamy wet wool, body odor mixed with deodorant—even from a distance, the girl's unique scent flooded Henry's nostrils. She reeked of stress. Her frantic shouts, her flailing arms, and her scent triggered something deep inside him. Suddenly, Henry itched to climb onto the jagged debris, to sniff the air as he moved over and around the chunks of snow, to follow his nose in search of hidden quarry.

In short, he wanted to do his job. And he wanted to do it *now.*

Ian halted him with a calmly uttered command. "Down, Henry. Down."

Henry immediately dropped to the snow between Ian's legs. As much as his drive to work was urging

★ 53 ★

him to *move-move-move*, it couldn't pull him away from Ian's control. His handler gave commands for a reason, and even though he might not understand what those reasons were right away, it never crossed his mind to disobey. So he settled more comfortably onto the cold snowpack while Ian spoke to the woman.

"Hey, it's okay, it's okay," he reassured her. "We're here to help."

Henry's ears pricked up. His handler's tone was kind and confident but firm, the same qualities it had when they were training together. But Ian's words weren't for him this time.

His eyes flicked to the woman. Her arms had stopped waving. Her shrieks had subsided. Her breath was coming in ragged sobs and her face was streaked with tears, but as Ian and the others began questioning her, Henry sensed that her anxiety was lessening.

After a quick back-and-forth with her, the ski patrollers circled up to talk together. Henry felt the woman looking at him and turned his honey-gold eyes to her. She took a step toward him and sank down onto her knees in the snow. Not so close that she could touch him, but near enough that he could hear her whisper.

"Hey there, boy. You're going to find him, right?" She bit her lip and stared up at the avalanche debris. "Please find him."

HECTOR

Dogs validated by CARDA specialize in locating victims buried by avalanches. But their training also prepares them for other rescue missions, including ground searches in missing persons cases. On New Year's Eve 2009, a snowboarder disappeared out-of-bounds on Mount Seymour, a small peak near Vancouver's North Shore. Local authorities searched for three days without finding him. That's when they called in Ian and his dog.

That dog wasn't Scout, but Ian's second CARDA dog, a black-and-white border collie named Hector. Ian brought him home in 2003, the year before Scout retired. After three years of training, Hector was validated. And three years after that, he and Ian put his searching skills to the test on Mount Seymour.

"Hector, an assistant ground searcher, and I were flown in by helicopter to the area where the snowboarder's track had last been seen," Ian recalls. "But the mountains around Vancouver are very rugged, and the rocky, snow-covered ground made it impossible for the pilot to land. So we got out of the helicopter by the hover-exit method, carefully climbing from the cabin to the skid and then lowering ourselves and our gear to the ground."

Once they were on the ground, Hector took over, tracking the snowboarder's scent as Ian and his assistant skied behind. "The missing man had left a confused path of footsteps everywhere, winding over, around, and through dense brush, downed logs, and debris," Ian remembers. "To be honest, the other searcher and I didn't have much hope of finding the snowboarder alive, not after three nights out in the freezing cold. But Hector made many critical decisions that kept us moving in the right direction. And he didn't give up, so we kept scrambling after him. After an hour, he led us to the missing man."

They summoned the helicopter for an emergency extrication. Hungry, delusional, and soaked through to the skin, the snowboarder was carefully loaded onto a stretcher lowered down from a helicopter.

The stretcher was hoisted up on a cable, then long lined up through a narrow gap in the trees and into the helicopter. Once on board, the snowboarder was flown to the nearest hospital.

Meanwhile, Ian, Hector, and the assistant set off to find an extrication point more suitable for a landing and pick up. Rather than return to their original starting point, they decided to look for a clearing nearer to their location. Their trek took them over challenging terrain that included the Seymour River. "At times we were wading up to our waists," Ian remembers.

They found what they thought was an acceptable spot, but the first extrication attempt almost ended in disaster. "I was standing in thigh-deep water among river boulders, watching the helicopter descend," Ian remembers. "That's when I realized we were in danger from a tail rotor strike. I had to wave off the pilot and abort the pickup."

They moved to a different location, where a second attempt via the hover method succeeded.

That rescue was Hector's big claim to fame and one of his last significant missions. "Avalanche search and rescue is really hard on canines," Ian says. Hector had been on the job for four years—not as long as Scout, but long enough for Ian to know Hector's working days were coming to a close.

It was time to start looking for another puppy to train.

SEVENTEEN MINUTES REMAINING...

Time was running out.

In a perfect world, Ian would have sent Henry off to search the second they were clear of the helicopter. But it wasn't a perfect world. The avalanche before them was proof enough of that. And sending Henry onto the debris field before questioning the young woman, their sole eyewitness to the event, would have been a mistake.

Searching was about eliminating the places where a person wasn't so the rescuers could focus their efforts on the places where the person might be. When they first disembarked from the helicopter, their search site encompassed the entire debris field. Not even Henry could cover that much terrain in the minutes they had left.

Vicky, the young woman, had provided them with vital information that narrowed their search field considerably. Moments before the avalanche swept him away, she said, her friend had been skiing midway down the left side of the slope. She gave a quick description of what he was wearing and his ski equipment. "He had a transceiver, too," she added, waving her hand at her own device in its harness.

Ian and the other searchers immediately consulted their own transceivers. If the missing man's device was sending out a signal, they should receive it. And then they could follow it to him.

But Ian's transceiver showed no evidence of a signal. From the grim looks on the others' faces, they hadn't picked it up, either. Maybe the man's beacon was still set on receive, not transmit. Maybe it had been damaged by the avalanche. Maybe there was a glitch in its software, or maybe it hadn't been working properly in the first place. In the end, the reason for the failure didn't matter. Not having a beacon just made their search a little more challenging.

Jan quickly scanned the debris field with her binoculars. "There," she said, pointing to the location where Vicky said her friend had vanished. "A fresh set of ski tracks. They cut off right at the edge of the slide."

The missing man wouldn't be at that exact spot, Ian knew, because the avalanche would have carried him farther down the slope. But those tracks confirmed Vicky's report and helped define their search zone even more.

"Right." Tom pulled out his avalanche probe and snapped it together. "I'll start at the bottom left and work my way up." He skied off toward the pile.

Vicky had been kneeling near Henry. When Tom set off, she rose to her feet. "Where's he going?"

"To do a hasty search," Ian replied. "A quick preliminary search of the target zone." Tom would systematically probe the snow and leave flags to mark potential buried finds. If he came across a ski or a pole or a glove, he'd give it a yank. In a best-case scenario, that item would still be attached to the missing man.

Ian turned to Jan. "Henry and I will enter at a midpoint below those ski tracks and move downward."

★63★

"You got the wind direction already?" Jan asked.

Ian nodded. The handful of snow he'd tossed in the air earlier had shown him it was blowing across the width of the avalanche. Knowing the direction of the wind was key to the success of Henry's search.

Unlike tracker dogs, who follow smells left by their target on the ground and nearby vegetation, Henry was trained to air scent—to sift through odors carried through the air. He was seeking a scent cone, the shape odors form as they fan out downward from their source. Scent is most concentrated at the cone's tip, where the source is located. If Henry intercepted even the weakest part of the scent cone, his super-sensitive nose would trace it back to the source—the buried victim.

Henry's best chance of intercepting that scent cone was to move perpendicular to the wind. If the wind had been blowing up or down the slope, Ian would have directed Henry to crisscross the target area horizontally. Since it was blowing sideways, he'd guide him in a top-to-bottom zigzag pattern.

"Good," Jan acknowledged. "Bob, you shadow Ian and Henry. Have your probe and shovel ready in case of a find."

"Can I do anything?" Vicky asked.

"Stay with me in case I have more questions for you. Your answers might help us find your missing friend faster."

Jan would also be mapping out the debris field, noting the location of any items sticking out of the snow that could point toward the missing man. And she'd be keeping careful watch on the terrain. At the first sign of danger, she'd alert the searchers to exit the debris—fast.

Bob shouldered his pack of gear. "Ready when you are, Ian."

Ian planted his poles in the snow and looked over at his dog lying patiently in the snow. "Henry!" he called. "This way!"

TRAINING GOALS

In the 1890s, a Russian scientist named Ivan Pavlov made an interesting discovery: dogs in his laboratory began salivating when a certain technician came into the room. The technician was in charge of feeding the dogs, so the dogs' response made sense. What intrigued Pavlov was that even when the technician didn't feed them, the dogs still salivated. They were responding to the *idea* of getting food, Pavlov realized, not the food itself.

Intrigued, Pavlov studied the behavior more closely. He set up experiments where he sounded a buzzer, then gave the dogs a treat. After enough repetitions, the dogs began salivating at the sound of the buzzer—even if they didn't receive food afterward. They had been conditioned to connect the sound with food. Hearing the buzzer was now enough to produce their response.

Today, Ian uses a similar method, called marker or clicker training, at his own training facility, the Ian Bunbury Dog School. Like Pavlov's experiment, his approach pairs a distinct sound signal, or marker, with a reward, typically food treats, toys, and games of tug. Markers can be the click of a handheld clicker—hence the term *clicker training*—or a single word command. Ian uses the word *yes*.

The first training exercise is called "charging the mark." The trainer clicks the clicker or says yes, pauses briefly, and then gives the dog the reward. "After many repetitions, the dog shows he understands that a reward follows the mark," Ian says. "Then the real training can begin."

First up are simple behaviors like making eye contact, nose to hand touches, or positions like sit, stand, and down. When the dog performs the desired behavior, the trainer immediately marks the action, pauses, and then presents him with the reward. "When the dog hears the signal, he understands that what he just did is good and that a reward will follow," Ian says. "So he's motivated to keep doing it. When the dog is motivated, the handler is only limited by his imagination and the dog's physical capabilities."

It's important the dog learns that his behavior drives the presentation of the reward, not the other way around, Ian adds. "If you show him the reward first and then ask for a behavior, he might decide what you're offering isn't worth his effort. Or maybe there's a distraction that has more value to him than the reward. And what if you don't have his reward with you all the time? Your chances of getting him to do what you want go way down then, because he's learned to do the behavior after he's seen the reward. So, no reward equals no action."

As the dog matures, the trainer withholds the reward from time to time. "Doing so keeps the dog keen to perform. He learns that sometimes he gets nothing and sometimes he gets a reward or maybe even a lot of rewards. He'll continue to work hard for that possible jackpot!"

In the world of dog handling, reward-based marker training is considered "new school." There is also an "old school" method known as avoidance/escape training. Here, the dog is pressured by the trainer into doing the desired behavior or punished for failing to do what is expected of him. The dog learns to avoid or escape these negative reactions by performing the correct actions. While the avoidance/escape method can produce results, Ian and most search and rescue dog trainers prefer the positive, reward-based marker training.

"SAR dogs are expected and encouraged to be friendly toward humans and other animals," Ian says, "and marker training usually leads to that result. Dogs trained by the avoidance/escape method, on the other hand, can become stressed and neurotic by the pressure and possibility of punishments. Their behavior can be unpredictable. That's not what you want in a search and rescue dog."

But marker training isn't just for SAR dogs. "My goal as a trainer of dogs and their people is to improve the dynamics of their relationship. Positive, reward-based training is the foundation of that." He pauses and smiles. "Once your dog realizes that you represent the best things in life, there is no limit to the things you can do together."

FIFTEEN MINUTES REMAINING...

When Ian called his name, Henry leaped to his feet, sending an explosion of snow into the air around him. Every fiber of his being was singing the same tune: *It's go time.*

Following Ian's direction, he galloped up the slope, steering clear of Ian's and Bob's skis but not straying too far from the searchers. He stopped when they stopped. Scooted between Ian's legs when Ian gestured for him to come. Quivered with eager anticipation as Ian crouched and laid his hands on his back. And then—

"Search!"

That single, authoritative command unleashed the work drive Henry had been holding in check. He darted toward the debris field, climbed up through the chunks, then paused to look back at Ian.

"This way!" His handler waved his arm toward the toe of the slide.

The command and gesture set Henry off in the right direction. Nose in the air, he began picking out a path that followed the avalanche's track down the slope. His nostril receptors registered a vast and changing array of odors. Like a rapid-fire canine version of a memory-based card game, he instantaneously matched each smell to smells he had encountered thousands of times before—while on patrol with Ian, during training exercises, on hikes in the mountain wilderness, and every time he turned a patch of snow from white to yellow. *Dirt. Moss. Leaves. Animal droppings.*

He paired different scents to their humans, too. Bob's smell was easy to identify. With every breath, the young searcher exhaled the pungent aroma of tuna salad on wheat bread and nacho cheese–flavored chips, the meal he'd eaten just before the callout. Henry had been nearly overwhelmed by the smell—in a mouthwatering, wish-he-had-shared-his-food-with-me kind of way—both times Bob had held him in the helicopter. Ian's smell, an outdoorsy combination of wood smoke, sweat, and evergreen, was immediately recognizable. Henry could have picked it out of a crowd of hundreds and traced it back to his handler in seconds. Harder to detect because of the distance between them was the smell of Tom's shampoo, and even fainter but still perceptible, the coffee Jan had spilled on her turnout gear the day before and the hot, musky odor of Vicky's lingering stress.

As quickly as he identified these odors, Henry discarded them. Because he wasn't searching for the scent of someone he knew, of someone he could hear and see. He was seeking an unfamiliar odor of a person hidden beneath a thick pile of snow and ice.

So far, that scent had eluded him. But he knew it was there. Ian wouldn't have brought him here if it weren't.

"This way, Henry!"

At Ian's command, Henry turned about and made his way up the slope. Then back down again, moving in a long, winding zigzag from the avalanche's edge toward its interior. The uneven terrain was frigid and rough beneath his paws, but he was too intent on his task to notice. Too busy testing the air for that one important odor. With nimble agility, he navigated over and around the debris. A quick trot up to the top of an inclined block of rock-hard snow. A jump down onto a stretch of field littered with frozen lumps and snowballs. A scurry beneath a wide, thick slab that hung over his head like a low roof.

When he emerged from beneath the overhanging rock, for a split second, that slab blocked the wind wafting across the avalanche. When he stepped out from beneath it, a gust blew into his face. That gust carried a sprinkling of snowy powder—and a faint smell.

Henry halted. He sniffed the air. Once. Twice.

Yes.

The smell was weak, but it was there, and it was different from any he'd smelled that or any other day. And that made it something that demanded further investigation.

Now that he'd caught the scent, he put his nose closer to the ice-crusted surface. His quarry was beneath the snow, so his quarry's scent would be richest near the ground. He ranged about the debris in a random way, not his earlier zigzag pattern, nostrils twitching as he tried to zero in on the faint odor or, better yet, its source.

Another gust of wind buffeted his body. Unlike the first, it blew up from the avalanche's toe. And instead of carrying the new, unfamiliar but wildly intriguing smell to Henry's nose, this gust and the bluster that followed stole that smell away.

Confused, he paused and straightened. He swung his head one way, then the other, nostrils working furiously as they combed the air.

But it was no use. The scent had vanished.

HENRY THE PUPPY

The first time Ian saw Henry in person was at the airport. "The breeder sent photos of him," he recalls, "and video of his parents and a copy of his pedigree, which listed two champion sheep herders in his lineage. So I was pretty confident Henry was the right dog for me."

Still, he wasn't 100 percent sure until the two were finally face-to-face. Then, one look was all it took. "There he was, this adorable little seven-week-old puppy who had just spent the last eight hours in the cargo hold of a plane. So he's got to be more than ready to get out of his crate, eat something, run, play, do his business, whatever, right? And I'm just some guy he's never met. But still, he's gazing up at me with this trusting expression, like, 'Hi, Dad!'" Ian shakes his head and smiles. "We connected right then and there."

Their initial bond strengthened in the hours that followed. "I took him from the airport to a park so he could run around. Back home, I fed him tidbits of raw steak. And he slept in a crate beside my bed that first night." Ian pauses. "And every night after, actually."

A strong bond between handler and dog is crucial for all canine search and rescue teams. In Ian's opinion, the strongest relationship is forged from equal parts love, respect, and engagement. "A dog can love you, but if it doesn't respect you or engage with you, it won't always follow your commands," he points out.

To build their foundation, Ian spent hours every day roaming the slopes of Whistler Mountain with Henry at his side. Not on skis or a snowmobile, though. Henry was born in mid-April and came to Ian at the beginning of June, when Ian was working for Whistler's summer patrol doing trail maintenance and going on emergency callouts for hikers and bikers in need of aid. But the lack of snow didn't get in the way of their preparations for CARDA's spring assessment, Henry's first big step toward validation.

"Nature presents plenty of opportunities for training exercises," Ian notes. Crossing a moss-covered log gave Henry experience with navigating unstable surfaces like those he'd encounter in avalanche debris. When he wandered off trail out of Ian's sight, he learned to use the sound of Ian's footsteps crashing through the underbrush to stay tuned to his handler's whereabouts. And when Ian ducked out of sight behind a boulder, Henry realized he could point his nose in the air and sniff him out.

When summer turned to fall, Ian took Henry for a short stint at a highly respected dog obedience school in California. There, Henry learned to follow Ian's hand and arm gestures along with simple commands. He also learned that responding properly to each signal yielded him a reward. That made him even more eager to perform well.

New experiences came that winter, too: his first snowfall, his first run between Ian's skis, and his first ride in the snowmobile driver's seat. With each passing week, his bond with Ian solidified and Ian's confidence in his puppy grew. When the snow melted away into springtime, Ian knew Henry, now one year old, was ready for his CARDA assessment.

The three-day May session was held on the shores of Okanagan Lake in British Columbia. Day one was orientation, when the instructors outlined what the recruits would be doing the next two days. On day two, Ian and Henry and five other dog-and-handler pairs headed to the training area to get their first look at the terrain. "I was checking for potential hazards like bees' nests, tree stumps, and holes in the ground, and for distractions like dead wildlife and cow patties. Dogs find those smelly things practically irresistible. I didn't want Henry running off to roll in one."

Once everyone had the lay of the land, the instructors assigned each team a slot in the testing lineup. Ian and Henry were second, so while the first pair was put through their paces, Henry and the other canines rested in their crates.

CARDA's spring assessment typically consists of games of runaway; basically, the dog must find a person who runs and hides. First up is master runaway. Here, the person hiding is the dog's handler. To encourage the dog to look for the handler, they play tug-of-war with the dog's favorite tug toy. When the dog is all revved up and fully engaged with the toy, the handler takes control of the toy, then runs away and disappears behind a blind—a wall or mound of snow big enough for the handler to hide behind—while another person holds the dog back. When the handler is out of sight, the dog is released and—hopefully—finds the handler.

The drills become increasingly difficult. After

basic master runaway comes master runaway with time delay, where the dog is held back for a greater length of time. Then master runaway with direction change, where the handler switches direction midway to the hiding spot. In order to follow the scent, the searching dog has to change direction, too. Lastly, a stranger takes the handler's place. After each successful find, the dog is rewarded with an exuberant game of tug-of-war. How exuberant?

"There's an old CARDA saying," Ian says. "'If you're not acting like an idiot, you're doing it wrong.'"

The first dog's runaway drills took half an hour to complete, after which the instructors debriefed the handler on his canine's performance. Had the dog displayed eagerness, energy, and persistence? Did it use its nose to search, not its eyes and ears? Tick all the boxes, Ian knew, and the dog would pass. Miss even a few, and the handler would be advised that his dog was likely ill-suited for the work—or that the dog had been scrubbed outright.

The first dog passed, and then it was Henry's turn. Ian had been through the process with Scout and Hector, so he played his part well. And he believed Henry had, too, until the debriefing.

"Henry had no problems," Ian says, "except one. His enthusiasm for 'ragging'—that tug-of-war game—wasn't as strong as the other dogs'." He shrugs. "But that's as much to do with the breed as Henry himself. Border collies are lovers, not fighters. They're bred to herd and protect animals, so the instinct to attack, to rip into something, even if it's just a toy, isn't as developed as it is in, say, a German shepherd being trained for police work. And Henry, by nature, is a calm dog. So that urge was even less in him."

In the end, Henry's calmness didn't stand in his way. He passed the assessment and was cleared to continue down the path to validation.

"It was a real leap of faith when I decided to take and train Henry without meeting him first," Ian acknowledges. "All dogs are different, just like people. Scout was super serious. Hector was a lovable clown."

And Henry? "He's a hard worker, beautifully behaved, and very smart. Maybe his calm demeanor wouldn't suit another handler. But he's always been the perfect fit for me."

TEN MINUTES REMAINING...

"Henry!"

Ian's call rang out through the valley as he crunched a few steps over the debris toward his dog. When Henry whipped his head around to look at him, Ian swept his arm toward the avalanche's right side. "This way!" He watched with satisfaction as Henry wheeled about and set off across the slope.

As a rule, Ian took a hands-off approach to Henry during a search. If he guided his dog with commands and gestures every step of the way, then Henry might refuse to work without his constant encouragement. Better to let his dog follow his instincts and his nose than to act as his cheerleader, Ian believed.

But when the wind suddenly changed direction and Henry hesitated, staying silent wasn't an option. His dog had been showing interest—that is, giving signs that he'd caught a whiff of a noteworthy scent. The changes in his movements—wandering over a small area with his nose to the snow instead of trotting onward with his nose sniffing the air— were subtle but unmistakable signals of that interest. Hopefully that scent was coming from the missing skier and not an article of clothing or another lost item saturated with the victim's smell. Either way, redirecting his dog to move against the grain of the wind gave him the best chance of picking up the scent again. Then it would be up to Henry to decide if it was really worth pursuing.

With the skier's time running out, Ian fervently hoped that proved to be the case. Or even better, that Henry jumped from showing interest to showing indication. If interest was mild curiosity, indication was total and complete absorption—the kind of absolute, unbreakable focus some humans had while playing their favorite video game. In human terms, interest was like channel surfing for a television show. Indication, on the other hand, was like binge-watching an entire season of that show—total and complete absorption.

Ian's thoughts were interrupted by Tom's voice over the radio. "Jan, you got our witness nearby?" The senior rescuer's hasty search had taken him to the center of the debris. He held a flag used to mark a find in one hand, but his gaze was aimed at the right edge of the slide.

"Affirmative," Jan said. "What's up?"

"Ask her if she saw anyone else when the avalanche hit," Tom said. "Because I might be looking at a second set of tracks."

"Hang on."

Ian kept his eyes on Henry as Jan quickly relayed the question to Vicky. The possibility of a second victim was daunting. It meant they'd have to divide their efforts between two search sites. Bob would head to the new area and begin a hasty search of his own. Ian, Henry, and Tom would continue to probe and search their original locations. With Henry's skilled nose leading the way and the fact that he'd already shown interest, Ian believed they stood a good chance of finding Vicky's friend before it was too late. But another skier, too? He shook his head.

★ 85 ★

By his watch, there were now less than eight minutes remaining in the thirty-minute countdown. Unless Bob discovered the second victim right away, Ian put the odds of that victim's survival at close to zero.

Jan came back on the radio. "Negative on the second skier!" she said. "Vicky had eyes on the slope just before the avalanche released and is sure no one else but she and her friend were there. I'll double-check that no one else was registered for backcountry in this area, but I'm looking at the tracks through my binoculars now, and they look windswept and worn down, not fresh and clean. I'd say they're a few days old, maybe more."

Ian let out a long, relieved breath and lifted his radio to his mouth. "Good news," he started to say. But before he did, he saw something that made his eyes widen and his heartbeat speed up.

Henry.

His dog had been maneuvering over the debris near where he'd shown interest. While Jan was delivering her report, Henry stepped onto an unstable slab of snow. The slab rocked forward. Henry scrabbled to find his footing but slipped off. He landed awkwardly on a pile of hard, round lumps of snow and fell over sideways. He sprang right back up, unharmed. Ian waited for his dog to resume his search pattern.

But in that split second, Henry's entire demeanor changed significantly. His body stiffened. His tail stopped waving. And he began to move with new purpose.

That's when Ian knew: Henry was onto something.

No, not something. Some*one*.

"Thatta boy, Henry," he whispered. He made no move to follow. Not yet. Not until Henry's actions told him to. "Go get him!"

HENRY'S FIRST WINTER COURSE

Border collies are bred to work. If they're inactive for long stretches of time, they get antsy. So the summer after Henry's spring assessment, Ian made sure his dog was busy every day. But not with strict formal training.

"I said to myself, *This is my dog's off-season. I'm going to give him the summer off from work*," Ian says. "Of course, he didn't realize it wasn't the same as always because he doesn't know the difference between work and play. But I knew we were going to have fun."

Ian took Henry on long hikes and for swims in mountaintop lakes. He took him canoeing and let him run through the forest when he went mountain biking. He watched Henry leap on top of boulders and race across Whistler Mountain's sky bridges. Whatever outdoor activity there was to do, he and Henry were doing it—and loving it all.

And whether Henry knew it or not, he was honing his search and rescue skills.

"I took him on a four-hour hike one day," Ian remembers. "He was roaming around off trail and out of sight in the underbrush as he often does. I didn't need to see him to know he was keying off my motions, keeping me in range. That awareness of my presence is what I want him to have during an avalanche search, so I never call him to me when he's off on his own unless I have to."

After ranging far afield for much of the hike, Henry suddenly appeared at Ian's side. An old glove was dangling from his mouth. "If I had ever had any doubt that he was search and rescue dog material," Ian says, "it vanished that moment. Not just because he'd found the glove, but because he recognized that the glove didn't belong in the environment where we were hiking. And because he felt compelled to show it to me. That's what search and rescue dogs do."

The following January, Ian was ready to show everyone else that Henry was a search and rescue dog at CARDA's winter course at Kicking Horse Mountain Resort in Golden, British Columbia. It was Henry's first winter session, but unlike other first-time dogs who were hoping to leave with their "In Training" certificates, Henry had a chance to head home with his full validation if he performed well.

Ian was the reason for the difference. "Because I'd had two dogs validated before, I held the rank of Senior Handler. That meant CARDA was prepared to validate Henry rather than draw out his training for another year. Of course, they had to like what they saw in him."

They did like what they saw. Henry was validated without a problem, and he and Ian were off and running as the newest CARDA team at Whistler. While they didn't get called out to any avalanches that season, they went out on ski patrol duty together daily throughout the winter. When Ian gave talks to schoolchildren, which he often did, he made sure Henry was included. "Kids loved seeing him jump on my back, and they liked it even better when I let him jump up on theirs," he says.

They trained regularly throughout the spring and summer, too. When the snow first started to fly in late fall, that training became more focused. CARDA requires teams to revalidate every year. To make sure Henry was ready, Ian spent the weeks leading up to the test putting his dog through various search and rescue exercises.

The test took place at Whistler in midwinter 2015. It wasn't during the weeklong general winter course, but at a smaller one-day revalidation-only event known as a roadside. The test consisted of two parts, the search and rescue exercises and the obedience exam.

The search and rescue came first. To pass, Henry had to locate three articles of clothing that were saturated with another handler's scent. To prepare the articles, the handler slept with or in the clothing for a few weeks prior to the test. The day before the drill, Ian and the handler buried two of the articles at the required depth of eighty centimeters (approximately thirty inches), then marked the locations with colored wands.

The third article, a backpack with a heavily scented rag tied to the outside, was buried and marked with a wand an hour before the test. Known as the "hot item," the pack was meant to simulate the smell of an avalanche victim. Ideally, Henry would find the "victim" first and then the other two articles.

At test time, the CARDA instructor noted the

burial places of the three items on a map, then pulled the wands from the snow. Shortly afterward, Henry and Ian arrived, and the test began.

Unfortunately, things didn't go quite as Ian hoped they would.

Bad conditions at the test site—old, hard snowpack and icy spots—made the course challenging for all the dogs. Even so, Henry found the hot item and one of the overnight articles without too much difficulty. But for some reason, the other overnight item eluded him.

Or did it?

"Henry indicated on a spot—that is, he dug at the snow and showed other signs that the article was buried in a particular location," Ian remembers. "But according to the instructor's map, the article was in a different place."

The instructor told Ian to call Henry off, then probed at the spot he'd marked on his map. To his consternation, he didn't find anything. A second instructor probed the area, too. Nothing. Then, when Henry was released for another attempt, he returned to his original spot and indicated again.

"I wasn't sure what to think at that point," Ian says. "On the one hand, I trusted my dog and the training I'd given him. But on the other, there was the instructor insisting that the third item was buried where he'd been probing. Who was right?"

In the end, who was right didn't matter—not to the instructors, anyway. According to their information, Henry had repeatedly indicated at the wrong spot. That meant he failed his revalidation.

"I was pretty dismayed," Ian admits. "The instructors' decision is final. That left me with a tough decision. I could scrub Henry from the program and start over with another dog. Or I could work with Henry some more and try for revalidation again later in the season."

Before he made up his mind, Ian decided to give Henry the benefit of the doubt. "I couldn't shake the feeling that he was right. So three days later, I returned to the search site and let him try again. And guess what? He indicated at the same spot. When I dug there, sure enough, I found the third article right where he'd said it was during the test. That made my decision easy: Henry was a dog worth sticking with."

Henry tested again that spring—and this time, he passed. As Ian had trusted he would.

FIVE MINUTES REMAINING...

This way!

The command came not from Ian, but from Henry's pink nose. It had lost the scent before. Now his nostril receptors had picked up a faint whiff again. They locked onto the odor, and Henry followed wherever they led.

This way. No, stop. Turn back. Now move forward. Ah. Good. Stronger again. This is the right way. Not that way. This way!

Even as Henry navigated over the snowy, debris-choked terrain in pursuit of the scent, he remained aware of the activity around him. Of Tom poking his avalanche probe into a small, jagged cluster of icy lumps and of Bob wheeling his arms as he teetered on an unstable chunk. Of Jan lowering her binoculars and jotting something in her notebook, and of Vicky shifting from foot to foot and hugging herself. Of Ian stopping in his tracks, arms folded and eyes watching. He was aware of the sounds they made, too—the crunch of their footsteps, the gentle *whsk-whsk* of turnout gear fabric rubbing together as they moved, the clank of Bob's shovel as it struck the concrete-hard snow. Their murmurs and radio chatter and breathing. He was aware of their unique smells, each one painting a vivid picture of its owner in his mind's eye. He was aware that the change in the wind's direction brought with it the promise of more snow.

Aware of it all. But distracted by none.

This way!

The scent was stronger now, minty toothpaste and floral laundry detergent mingled with foot odor and stale underarm sweat. It flowed over and around him, enveloping him. If the smell had been a flashlight beam, he would have been blinded by the brilliance.

Body and tail tense with anticipation, eyes picking

out a trail through snowy rubble, nose hovering over the ground and hoovering up the scent, he pursued the odor on the breeze.

This way!

With every footfall he took in the right direction, the scent grew more intense, and he grew more excited. He no longer zigzagged in wide curving arcs through the chunks but trotted steadily forward, his red furry body in its bright red-and-black vest a stark contrast to the white snow. Laser focused. Confident. Driven.

This way! This—

He passed a low mound of snow, and the scent suddenly disappeared. He whirled around and retraced his steps, refusing to let the smell slip away from him again. Six paces took him back to the mound. He circled it, then froze by a thin crack in the snow-dusted crust. One whiff there, and his nostril receptors lit up like a pinball machine. That's when his brain took over from his nose to issue a new command.

Dig!

His paws obeyed, working furiously at the crack. The crust resisted the assault. He shifted to a different side and attacked from another angle.

★**97**★

Dig!

His front claws dislodged a small shard of ice and snow. He flung it back through his hind legs, along with a flurry of powder, and scrabbled at the crack some more. A second shard popped loose, and a hole no wider than his tail opened up. From it, the overpowering scent of his quarry flooded his nose and boosted him into overdrive.

Dig-dig-dig-dig-dig!

Frenzied but not frantic, Henry scratched and clawed and dug. The hole widened enough for him to shove his nose inside. He drank in the scent in one deep inhalation, then backpedaled and barked. Out of the corner of his eye, he saw Ian heading toward him. He lunged back to the hole and raked at the opening with greater vigor. A mini-blizzard whipped up behind his tail as he tossed chunks of ice and snow between his legs.

So close! So close! Dig-dig-di—

Crunch!

His paw punched through the hole. Pieces of the surrounding surface collapsed inward, and suddenly the opening was large enough for him to fit through. With a throaty growl of triumph, he darted forward

★98★

into the hole, bringing down another shower of ice crystals and powdery snow with him.

And inside that snowy enclosure ripe with the smell of mint and detergent and feet and underarm sweat he found his quarry at last.

But the mission wasn't over. There was still one very crucial thing left to do.

HENRY AND THE ADVANCED WINTER COURSE

It's every backcountry skier's nightmare: an avalanche sweeps them, their friend, or their whole group over a cliff into a deep crevasse. And it's every ski patroller's worst-case scenario, too. Mounting a search and rescue mission in the backcountry, especially in the mountains of British Columbia, is a serious challenge. With its steep drop-offs, jagged outcrops, and huge icy glaciers, the terrain can be hard to maneuver in the best conditions. In frigid wintry weather, it can be downright treacherous, even deadly. Only those with the right skills, gear, and team stand a chance of success.

That's why Ian and Henry work as hard as they do. And it's why they participate in CARDA's most strenuous and exciting training session, the advanced winter course.

Revalidation is one small part of the course and is

typically taken care of the first day. So what do they do during the rest of the session?

"A better question might be, what *don't* we do?" Ian says. "On the second morning, we fly by helicopter to a remote part of Whistler or one of the other ski resorts in British Columbia. For the next several days, we winter camp. Sometimes we have huts to protect us from the elements, but other times we just have portable shelters. And one time we were told to leave our gear at home and build our own shelters!

"Once we're settled in, we work on our winter survival skills. We do whiteout navigation, which is learning to keep our bearings in bad snowstorms. We do snowpack study skills, where we get a better understanding of what conditions could lead to avalanches. There's even something called advanced shoveling techniques. Seriously, that's a thing!"

One of the primary skills the dog-and-handler teams practice is how to travel in a column up a glacier or steep snowy incline while connected by a rope. "The handlers are roped together on skis with their dogs attached to the line right behind them. The dogs are supposed to follow their handlers. But that's hard to learn. So it's quite common for the teams to get tangled up when a dog tries to go around and get ahead of its handler."

Dogs sometimes climb on the tails of their handlers' skis, too, which can lead to everyone ending up in a heap. "I remember hearing one of the other handlers declare, 'My goal for the day is to not yell at my dog!'" Ian says.

In addition to practicing these skills—and trying not to get tangled, tripped up, frustrated, or all three—the handlers and their dogs take on challenging avalanche search and rescue scenarios. For one exercise, they stage a Code A in a crevasse filled with avalanche debris. One group of handlers accesses the debris from the bottom, burying scented articles, ski equipment, and even food in the rock-hard snow. Meanwhile, on the cliff above, two handlers stand at either end of a line. In the middle is a dog attached to the line by his harness. Using a system of pulleys and carabiners and their own body weight, the handlers slowly lower the dog down to the pile.

Once there, the dog remains on the line while conducting the search. "We want to be able to pull the dog out if we need to," Ian says. "The idea is to get used to the feel of being attached to the rope in case we ever use this technique."

Oftentimes, another dog or two will join the search. More dogs mean more territory is being covered, which, in a real-life situation, could result in the victim being found sooner.

There's another reason for more canines to work at the same time. "Other dogs can be a huge distraction. Learning to ignore them is a big part of the canine's training," Ian says. "Henry has mastered that skill. To him, most people and dogs are like furniture—there, but not something to be bothered by."

Henry isn't bothered by being lowered off the side of a cliff, either. "Once his feet leave the ground, he's just hanging out, no big deal," Ian says.

The same is true when he's dangling below a helicopter on a long line. Most CARDA teams will never need to access a rescue site by long line. But they practice the maneuver just in case.

"The drill starts on the ground, not in the air as some people think. The line is laid out in a wide zigzag from the front of the helicopter. The handler straps into a harness attached to the line, and his dog clips to him in his own harness, just like when we rappel down a cliff together. When everyone is secure, the helicopter takes off, the line tightens, and *voom!* Handler and dog lift off the ground and into the air.

"Sometimes I hold Henry, but usually, he just hangs against my body," Ian adds. "I always appreciate how calm he is, because when we're in the air, we have to remain still so we don't impact the helicopter's flight. That doesn't mean we're not moving. There have been times when we're slowly spinning the whole time we're flying. It's like being on a carnival ride."

As challenging mentally and physically as the advanced winter course is for both handler and dog, Ian usually manages to carve out some special time with Henry. "One of my favorite things to do is ski down a big powder slope with Henry by my side. After the slow trudge up the hill, we get to the top. I remove my climbing skins, maybe have a snack and some water, then step back into my bindings. That's when Henry knows for sure we're not going uphill anymore. His excitement matches mine as I point my skis downhill and push off. As I pick up speed, my mind automatically calculates everything about the run ahead. How much effort will I need? How deep is the snow? Did I wax right? What kind of turns will I do?

"Then I look over at Henry running alongside me. And it strikes me: to him, none of those details matter. The only thing is the here and now, the pure joy of the wind and the snow in his face. Suddenly, I'm feeling that, too. I become like Henry, carefree and living in the moment."

Ian smiles then and reaches over to pat Henry's head. "I think every handler would agree: it's times like that that make all our hard work worthwhile."

TWO MINUTES REMAINING...

Here we go.

Ian thundered up just as Henry plunged into the snow cave. Seconds later, his dog's hindquarters reappeared, and Henry began backing out. Not all at once, but with small jerking motions as he yanked something out with him.

Something...and someone: a young man in a bright blue ski parka and black ski pants. The man dragged himself out of the cave with one arm, gasping with every movement.

They were not gasps of pain, however, but of laughter. And his one-armed crawl was because he held tight to a tug toy—an old knit scarf with knots tied at intervals down its length—with his free hand.

Henry's teeth were sunk into the other end. Eyes shining with glee and a hint of mischief, he yanked again, hard enough for the man to lose his grip.

"Oh, Henry, you rascal!" The man's name was Jay, and though he had been buried in the snow for nearly half an hour, he had never been in any danger. A fellow CARDA handler, he had volunteered to play the role of "quarry" so Ian, Henry, and the other searchers could take part in an elaborate training exercise. Jay and Vicky, another volunteer, had arrived at the site earlier that day to bury articles of unwashed clothing saturated in Jay's scent throughout the debris field. They also dug out a snow cave for Jay to hide in.

Ian noted that they'd followed his cave design, carving out a well for Jay's feet, a bench for him to sit on, and plenty of head room. Such a cave took more time to make, but the alternative was reclining on your back with your face inches from the snow ceiling. Ian had a touch of claustrophobia—the fear of being enclosed in small, tight spaces—that came from the knowledge of what being trapped in the

★108★

snow could do to a person. Sitting upright alleviated any panic he felt when he played the victim.

When everything on the avalanche site was ready, Vicky, the avalanche's "witness," had called dispatch to report the slide. Then she quickly helped Jay wall himself inside the cave with jagged chunks of snow before ducking behind a huge block of debris to await the helicopter and rescue team's arrival.

A lot more preparation had gone into the exercise than just hiding Jay and his clothes. The avalanche had been purposefully triggered two days before. That morning, Jan triple-checked it for hang fire. If she'd spotted any hazard, she would have canceled the exercise just as she would have canceled a real search. While Ian and Henry attended their duties on the mountain, ski patrollers in the bump room monitored the weather forecast leading up to the callout. Any hint of a storm hitting during the time of the drill, and the exercise would have been postponed. The area itself was cordoned off to prevent skiers from entering, both for their own safety and to avoid any unnecessary distraction to the searchers.

As carefully staged as the exercise was, there were still a few unexpected turns along the way. The pilot choosing to practice his toe-in maneuver rather than landing, for instance—that had taken Ian by surprise. The sudden shift in the wind's direction, too—the weather forecast hadn't mentioned that possibility.

Some might have grumbled about the changes, but Ian welcomed them. Developments like that made the training more authentic. In a real search, unforeseen challenges were very likely to crop up. The more he and the other searchers practiced adjusting and adapting to new conditions, the better they'd be when an actual search and rescue threw obstacles in their path.

Not that those obstacles had stopped Henry. He'd performed like the champ he was, and now he deserved his reward. Not food—that would come later—but a celebration.

Ian swept in and captured the free end of the scarf. A mile-wide smile on his face, he wrestled with his dog while gently thumping Henry's head, shoulders, back, and hindquarters with vigorous, loving pets and showering him with glowing praise. "Good boy, Henry! Good boy!"

"Who's a good dog?" Jay echoed in a singsong voice. "You are, Henry! You are!"

★110★

Henry clenched his jaws on the scarf, dug his paws into the snow, and pulled once, twice, three times. Then he paused, laid a paw on top of the gnarled fabric, and stared up at Ian. Goading him. Ian laughed and gave the toy a quick yank, sparking another wrestling match.

He relinquished the tug toy when Jan, Tom, Bob, and Vicky joined them. Jan held up her arm and showed them her watch. "15:04," she reported with satisfaction. The others gave a cheer. They'd beaten the thirty-minute countdown by a full two minutes!

"And I think we all know who to thank for that result," Jan added.

All eyes turned to Henry. The little red-and-white border collie was lying in the snow at Ian's feet, happily gnawing the sodden scarf. When their attention swung his way, he dropped the tug toy and looked up. His gaze flicked over each of them in turn.

His honey-gold eyes found Ian last of all. His mouth opened in a panting canine grin. His ears pricked forward as his handler knelt beside him.

"Good dog, Henry." Ian pressed his cheek to Henry's furry forehead. "Such a good dog."

THE FIVE DEADLIEST AVALANCHES IN HISTORY

Avalanche forecasting and control measures are key to predicting and preventing harmful slides. But slides can occur even in carefully monitored avalanche-prone areas. And if one of those unexpected slides hits in a populated region, the result spells disaster.

The following pages catalog some of the worst avalanches ever recorded.

#5

When: 1950–1951
Where: The Alps bordering Switzerland and Austria
Trigger: An abnormal weather pattern that dumped ten to fifteen feet of heavy snow in just three days
Number: 649 separate slides
Hardest Hit: Austria
Death Toll: 265
More About This Event: More than 40,000 people are believed to have been buried in snow during the three-month-long Winter of Terror. It's tragic that 265 of those people perished, but remarkable that so many more survived.

#4

When: February 24–28, 2015

Where: Panjshir Province, Afghanistan

Trigger: Heavy snowfall, resulting in unstable snow-pack

Number: 40 reported slides

Hardest Hit: Panjshir Valley

Death Toll: 310

More About This Event: This mountainous region of northeast Afghanistan has a history of tragic avalanches. In early February 2010, 165 travelers lost their lives when multiple slides overwhelmed them on roadways and in the Salang Tunnel. Three large avalanches struck remote villages in March 2012. More than 50 people died.

#3

When: January 10, 1962
Where: Mount Huascarán, Peru
Trigger: The release of an enormous glacier from the mountaintop
Size: 6 million tons of ice and rock
Hardest Hit: The villages of Ranrahirca and Huarascucho
Death Toll: 4,000
More About This Event: Avalanches regularly plagued the villages at the base of Mount Huascarán. Usually, residents had twenty to thirty minutes after the sound of ice cracking to escape. This time, the slide took just seven minutes to cover nine and a half miles—which didn't give villagers nearly enough time to evacuate before their communities were buried beneath forty feet of snow, ice, and debris.

#2

When: December 1916
Where: Mount Marmolada, Italy
Trigger: Unusually heavy snowfall followed by a sudden thaw, resulting in unstable snowpack
Size: 200,000 tons of snow, rock, and ice in the first slide alone
Hardest Hit: Austrian and Italian military barracks located in the Italian Alps
Death Toll: 9,000–10,000
More About This Event: Not a single event, but a series of devastating avalanches that occurred over several days took the lives of Austrian and Italian soldiers fighting on opposite sides of World War I. Some later claimed the slides were set off by the soldiers themselves to wipe out their enemies. But the dangerous conditions were the more likely culprit. How the initial disaster, which took place on Wednesday, December 13, came to be known as "White Friday" is a mystery.

#1

When: May 31, 1970

Where: Mount Huascarán, Peru

Trigger: A powerful undersea earthquake that jarred a glacier from the mountaintop

Size: 16 billion tons of snow, ice, and rock

Speed: 135–270 mph

Hardest Hit: Villages of Yungay and Ranrahirca

Death Toll: 20,000–25,000

More About This Event: Three hundred children from Yungay were attending a circus outside their village when the earthquake hit. Before the glacier-driven avalanche raced down the mountainside, a quick-thinking circus clown led them to higher ground. Today, May 31 is Peru's National Disaster Education and Reflection Day in honor of those who were not as fortunate.

EPILOGUE

Saving a life is the mission of every CARDA team. That's why Henry and Ian and other dog-and-handler pairs train constantly to hone their skills. They know that someday, they might be the reason a person gets to celebrate another birthday.

Avalanche callouts are rare. But sadly, rescues are even rarer. In fact, since CARDA's founding in 1984, there has been just one live find in Canada.

It happened on December 19, 2000. Ryan Radchenko was skiing in an out-of-bounds area of Fernie Alpine Resort in British Columbia when an avalanche hit and buried him. CARDA handler Robin Siggers and his dog Keno, a Labrador retriever–border collie mix, responded to the callout. Minutes after arriving on the scene, Keno zeroed in on Ryan's scent and traced it to its source.

"He's trained to dig like crazy when he finds a person," Siggers told a reporter. "About a foot below the surface, he uncovered Ryan's hand."

Ryan survived his avalanche ordeal, but the truth is, most avalanche callouts end as recoveries—when, after too much time has passed for the victim to possibly have survived, the goal becomes to find the body of the missing person. "That's an incredibly important goal," Ian says. "Parents, siblings, relatives, friends, acquaintances—everyone suffers when an avalanche claims a life. Having their loved one's remains returned to them helps them cope with their loss. It gives them a sense of closure."

On March 4, 2017, Ian and Henry were able to give that closure to a local family.

"It was just before noon," Ian recalls, "and Henry and I were outside the Alpine Service Building giving a presentation about avalanche rescue dogs to a group of middle school kids. Then a call came in."

An avalanche had occurred half an hour earlier in the remote Hanging Lake region of Whistler Mountain. Witnesses reported that a skier was missing.

★120★

Ian and Henry—both in their gear, ready as always in case of a Code A—dropped everything and went into action.

They met up with the rest of the rescue team at the helipad. "Clouds and fog made the flight to the slide difficult," Ian says. "Without the skill and local knowledge of the pilot, insertion would have been nearly impossible."

The helicopter landed in deep powder near the top of the avalanche slide at Hanging Lake. By then, friends of the missing skier and others who witnessed the disaster, close to thirty people in total, had been combing the site for more than an hour. Though no one said it out loud, most probably recognized that after that much time, the rescue mission had changed to one of recovery.

Henry got to work immediately. He stayed on task despite the distraction of numerous people ranging over the site. He barely even paused when another dog, untrained and unsecured, ran onto the debris. An hour passed. The weather cleared, bringing bright afternoon sunshine. Some of the witnesses, exhausted and discouraged, trickled away from the site. But Henry kept searching. The only time he slowed was when the wind stopped blowing. As an air scent dog, he relied on wind to carry odor to his nose. Without it, he was searching blind. And yet he still searched.

More time went by. The unrestrained dog was corralled and moved off-site. Additional trained rescuers arrived, including a second CARDA team who started searching in another part of the debris. But even with all that manpower focused on one goal, the missing skier's whereabouts remained a mystery.

Until Henry found him.

"He'd passed over the same patch of snow before and hadn't shown any interest," Ian remembers. "But the next time, he caught the scent. His body language changed. I know him so well; there was no question at all in my mind that he was indicating a find."

Tragically, the skier did not survive. But thanks to Henry, his loved ones could bring him home.

"Henry and I may never get another Code A callout before he retires," Ian says. "But if this was his only one…well, I couldn't be prouder of what he did that day. Of what he does *every* day. Some people who meet him might think he's just a well-trained dog with a chill personality. But to me, he's a Superpower Dog."

IAN'S CARDA DOGS

SCOUT: BLACK-AND-WHITE FLOPPY-EARED BORDER COLLIE

Scout as a puppy.

An older Scout with his (human) brother.

1993–2008

Validated: January 1995

Career: 1995–2004

Retirement: 2004

Notable achievement: Scout's successful career as Ian's first CARDA dog led to Ian's position as a Senior Handler.

HECTOR: BLACK-AND-WHITE PRICK-EARED BORDER COLLIE

Hector and Ian.

2003-2013

Validated: January 2006

Career: 2006-2010

Retirement: 2010

Notable achievement: Hector's diligent search for a missing snowboarder in January 2010 saved the man's life.

Henry on Whistler Mountain.

HENRY: RED-AND-WHITE PRICK-EARED BORDER COLLIE

2012-

Validated: January 2014

Career: 2014-

Retirement: Not yet!

Notable achievement: The recovery of an avalanche victim's remains on March 4, 2017—while not a live find, Henry's persistence gave the victim's loved ones closure.

SUPERPOWER DOG FACTS

ONE-IN-A-MILLION NOSE

Dogs can track a lost child's scent trail through a busy city area even forty-eight hours after the child has left. They can detect tiny quantities of drugs or explosives. They can even use their nose to detect avalanche victims buried in snow and help doctors diagnose certain types of cancer. The cells that are receptive to odors are called olfactory sensory neurons. Not only do dogs have many more of these sensory cells than we do, they also have a proportionately larger part of their brain dedicated to processing this information. Bloodhounds, for example, have millions more cells for odor detection than humans! Combine that with a brain capable of detecting a single odor hours after it was left behind, and you have a superpower.

A bloodhound on the scent of a missing person, or a trained dog helping to detect diseases, can detect a single molecule in a whole snout full of air. This is measured in something scientists call ppm, or parts per million. One scent molecule out of a million is enough to help dogs in search and rescue work.

Just how *small* is one part per million, or one ppm? Think about it in terms of grains of rice. Imagine dropping a green grain of rice into a single one-pound bag of rice, which contains about twenty thousand grains. You would need fifty bags of rice to get to one million grains—and your one green grain of rice would be hiding somewhere in that mess of grains. Can you imagine finding your one grain of rice in a sack that weighs as much as a six-year-old?

If that grain of rice was a scent molecule, our bloodhounds could find it in a sniff, thanks to a large part of their nose and a large part of their brain devoted to the job. Dogs have even been tested at identifying scents in the ppb (parts per billion) and ppt (parts per trillion) range.

DOGS AND TOYS

Dogs come in a wide variety of shapes and sizes, but they all need to play. Why do you think that is? Scientists have found that play helps keep your dog physically and mentally healthy, builds a bond of trust and understanding with your dog, and helps your dog learn. Some dogs even find play to be more of a reward than food.

SPEAKING A DOG'S LANGUAGE

Dogs don't have an easy way to communicate with humans, though their "language" can be learned over time. Dogs' ear movement, tail position, actions, and body language can all tell a story. Working dogs need their human partners to understand what they're trying to tell them, so the dogs communicate through their ears, eyes, tail, and whole body. Here are some hints of what dogs might be saying, based on their position or actions:

What a dog might be saying	When you see them with their...
I'm ready to listen to you.	Ears facing forward. Tail held upright. Head up with back straight.
I'm hearing something somewhere.	Ears facing to the sides.
I'm afraid.	Tail tucked between the legs. Back hunched with head tucked down.
I'm ready to play.	Tail wagging. Chest down with elbows flat on the ground and rump up.

Before petting or interacting with a dog for the first time, it's important to ask the dog's human companion for permission—not all dogs are comfortable with new people.

DOG DIFFERENCES

Did you know that dogs, as a group, are the most diverse (varied) kind of mammal? Hundreds of different types of purebred dogs are recognized worldwide, such as cocker spaniels, poodles, Labrador retrievers, pugs, and beagles. There are also countless numbers of "designer" dogs, or mixes of two purebreds, including the cockapoo, the labradoodle, and the puggle, plus other mixed-breed dogs that can be a combination of two or more breeds. These dogs have all inherited traits, such as head length, ear shape, and coat (fur) color and type, from their parents, grandparents, and other ancestors.

WHAT'S YOUR SUPERPOWER?

Think about the people in your life. Who would you go to for help with a tricky math problem? Who could suggest the best word for the story you're writing? Who will score the next goal in your soccer game?

Most people have a passion for certain subjects. We can quickly identify our own strengths or passions, and we can often identify the strengths of others from the following list: word strong, number strong, music strong, art strong, sports strong, nature strong, people strong, and self strong.

Over the past centuries, different dog breeds became good at different things, and dogs continue to be selectively bred in part to excel in those certain skills. We could consider them to be smelling strong, hearing strong, caregiving strong, bravery strong, energetic strong, retrieving strong, herding strong, swimming strong, and snow strong.

What are your superpowers? What are your dog's? How can you use those strengths to make the world a better place?

The authors invite dog owners to visit their website at superpowerdogs.com to share their dog's superpowers.

Em*bark* on adventures with real-life
SUPERPOWER DOGS
Stars of the **IMAX®** film!

A FULL-COLOR PHOTO BOOK FOR READERS OF ALL AGES!

Action- and fact-packed nonfiction adventures with bonus full-color photos

 LITTLE, BROWN AND COMPANY
BOOKS FOR YOUNG READERS

#SuperpowerDogs

LBYR.com

IMAX® is a registered trademark of IMAX Corporation.

Ian and Henry patrol the slopes, ready to help anyone in need.

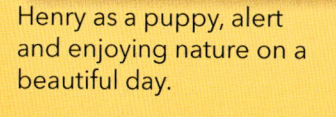

Henry as a puppy, alert and enjoying nature on a beautiful day.

Henry on a street that shares his name.

Henry and Khombu play at home.

Ian Cruickshank

In good times and bad, Henry and Ian have an unbreakable bond.

© 2019 by Cosmic Picture Limited

Ian and Henry take the lead as the CARDA dog-and-handler pairs race across the slopes.

© 2019 by Danny Wilcox Frazier VII, for Cosmic Picture Limited

The Bunbury family

Whether by skis, chairlift, snowmobile, or helicopter, on foot or paw, Henry and Ian have lots of ways to get around Whistler!

The Bunbury family

Henry waits in the CARDA team's chopper.

Henry and Ian are lowered from the helicopter to the mountain below.

© 2019 by Danny Wilcox Frazier VII, for Cosmic Picture Limited

Henry high atop Whistler Mountain in the winter…

…and in the summer

The Bunbury family

Henry races through the snow on high alert.

After Henry catches a scent, he'll bark, scratch,
and dig his way to the rescue.

The Bunbury family

Henry and Ian on Hanging Lake, a popular backcountry skiing site near Whistler Mountain.

© 2019 by Reed Smoot, for Cosmic Picture Limited

Hollywood comes calling! Henry strikes a pose with actor Chris Evans, the narrator of the movie *Superpower Dogs*.